SUBCUTANEOUSLY, MY DEAR WATSON

Subcutaneously, My Dear Watson

SHERLOCK HOLMES AND THE COCAINE HABIT

by

JACK TRACY

with

JIM BERKEY

Illustrated by

PAUL M. McCALL

*with Sidney Paget's original representations of Sherlock Holmes
and other turn-of-the-century illustrations*

**JAMES A. ROCK & COMPANY
PUBLISHERS** ◦◦◦◦◦◦◦◦**1978**

Hardbound ISBN: 0-918736-02-1
Paperbound ISBN: 0-918736-03-x

First Edition: June 1978

Printed in the United States of America

Acknowledgements

Grateful acknowledgement is extended to Dr. Roger Maickel, Head of the Pharmacology Section of the Medical Sciences Program (School of Medicine), Indiana University at Bloomington. Dr. Maickel entered into our little project with the proper spirit of Sherlockian whimsy, and offered many valuable insights into the pharmacology of cocaine, modern and historical. Needless to say, any conclusions reached in this book are those of the authors, who alone must bear responsibility for errors of fact or judgement.

Thanks are due also to John Hyzer, who carried out the fine rephotography of Victorian and Edwardian illustrations. And to the many folks at James A. Rock & Company who participated, in one way or another, in the production of this volume.

SUBCUTANEOUSLY,
MY DEAR WATSON

"He thrust the sharp point home. . ."

Sherlock Holmes took his bottle from the corner of the mantelpiece, and his hypodermic syringe from its neat morocco case. With his long, white, nervous fingers he adjusted the delicate needle and rolled back his left shirt-cuff. For some little time his eyes rested thoughtfully upon the sinewy forearm and wrist, all dotted and scarred with innumerable puncture-marks. Finally, he thrust the sharp point home, pressed down the tiny piston, and sank back into the velvet-lined arm-chair with a long sigh of satisfaction. . . .

"Which is it to-day," I asked, "morphine or cocaine?"

He raised his eyes languidly from the old black-letter volume which he had opened.

"It is cocaine," he said, "a seven-per-cent. solution."

IN those opening paragraphs of *The Sign of the Four,* published in 1890, the world was introduced to Sherlock Holmes, cocaine addict—perhaps the best known drug user of all time.

From its very beginning, Holmes's drug dependence seized the popular imagination. All the rest of his more bizarre idiosyncrasies—the cigars kept in the coal-scuttle and the noxious shag tobacco in the toe-end of a Persian slipper, the before-breakfast pipe "composed of all the plugs and dottles left from his smokes of the day before, all carefully dried and collected on the corner of the mantelpiece," his aversions to women and ventilated rooms, propensity for indoor pistol-practice, and habit of transfixing his unanswered correspondence to the mantel with a jack-knife — all came later, in the several series of short stories which began appearing in 1891. The cocaine was the first. It has always been the most intriguing and the least understood.

Not that Holmes's cocainism was calculated to shock Dr. Watson's Victorian readers. In those days every deadly substance from morphine to arsenic was readily and legally available without prescription at the neighbourhood chemist's. At best the cocaine use was a bit of romance dashed into Holmes's cold-blooded personality. At its worst, as one turn-of-the-century critic put it, it was "a curious touch."

But it wasn't long before attitudes were changing, and with them all objectivity toward Holmes's habit, especially in the United States, where the bulk of the stories' market now lay. With the coming of the new century, Watson avoided any mention of cocaine, except by implication, in his tales, and even inserted a spurious allusion in the story of *The Missing Three-Quarter* to the detective's having been "weaned" from his "drug mania."

Still, in the decades following the First World War, clergymen and educators denounced Holmes for his pernicious example, and the press frequently reported the tales' removal from school library shelves. "People get put in jail by a coke fiend. How could you trust this bum?" one prominent mystery writer is alleged to have sneered at Holmes. The great George Bernard Shaw dismissed him as "a drug addict without a single amiable trait." The low point was reached by members of the Baker Street Irregulars, the national association of Sherlock Holmes addicts, who in the 1940s began writing a series of articles suggesting that their "Master" was never a drug user at all, but merely feigned addiction either as a practical joke on the good Watson or as part of some involved scheme to lull his enemies into carelessness.

The reaction, when it inevitably came, has been even sillier. In the book and movie versions of Nicholas Meyer's *The Seven-Per-Cent Solution,* Holmes suffers the agonies of opiate withdrawal while throwing off his cocaine dependence. The promotional material for a recent re-release of 1939's *The Hound of the Baskervilles* touted Holmes as a "junkie cop" and implied that the film was censored originally because of its allusions to drugs. These lying advertisements prompted many parents to keep their children away from this first and best of the Basil Rathbone-Nigel Bruce interpretations, but CBS has since acquired and aired it. Over on NBC, Holmes's evident relish at lighting up his old clay pipe in the made-for-TV film *Sherlock Holmes in New York* caused some viewers, at least, to come away with the image of his actually *smoking* his dope in his meerschaum.

"Now, I make a point of never having any prejudices, and of following docilely wherever fact may lead me," Holmes himself declared. In among the conflicting biases of the moralists, the apologists, and the revisionists is to be found the real story of Sherlock Holmes and cocaine.

He perceived himself an accredited representative of the scientific community, devoted to the bold experiment and the practical demonstration.

THROUGHOUT his early life Holmes remained a forward-looking and liberal-minded "scientific" man who embraced radical philosophies, applauded reform, and devised a number of innovations in scientific crime detection. "One's ideas must be as broad as Nature if they are to interpret Nature," he remarked to Watson in *A Study in Scarlet*. He was just thirty years old when cocaine made its appearance on the Victorian drug scene in 1884.

He could scarcely avoid reading of the score of new surgical and therapeutic benefits then beginning to be claimed for the substance. He perceived himself an accredited representative of the scientific community, devoted to the bold experiment and the practical demonstration. He lived in an era when men experimented upon themselves as eagerly as upon their families, their friends, and their professional colleagues. And his chosen speciality was organic chemistry.

"I could imagine him giving a friend a little pinch of the latest vegetable alkaloid," an acquaintance said of Holmes as early as 1881, the traditional year for the events of *A Study in Scarlet*, "not out of malevolence, you understand, but simply out of a spirit of inquiry in order to have an accurate idea of the effects. To do him justice, I think he would take it himself with the same readiness." In the case of cocaine, that is precisely what he did.

Cocaine, in fact, *is* a vegetable alkaloid — $C_{17}H_{21}NO_4$ — the principal active ingredient in the leaves of the South American coca plant, *Erythroxylon coca.* For centuries, coca leaves were chewed by the Incas for their stimulant properties. They were brought to Europe by the Spanish early in the sixteenth century, but cocaine itself was not chemically isolated until at least 1844. Its commercial manufacture was begun in 1862, and in 1883 its medical applications first came to light when a Bavarian army doctor discovered its usefulness as an anti-fatigue agent. The following year it began to be used as a local anaesthetic, particularly in dentistry and ophthamology.

The drug came to the attention of the general public in 1884, when the writings of that ambitious young Viennese physician Sigmund Fréud precipitated a controversy over cocaine which soon spilled into the popular press. While the medical community at large quickly cautioned against the toxic and addictive properties of cocaine, Freud stubbornly defended it in his contributions to the medical literature, praising it as a "magical substance," prescribing it for a wide variety of ailments — from seasickness and gastric disorders to melancholia and the morphine habit — and in particular lauding its stimulant and anti-depressive effects. He took the drug himself, and having experienced no addictive symptoms he steadfastly denied that cocaine dependence was a serious consideration despite mounting evidence to the contrary, a position he did not abandon until late in 1887.

That year 1887 has a triple significance in Holmes's own life. In December, the story of Holmes and Watson's meeting and first case together, *A Study in Scarlet,* was published in *Beeton's Christmas Annual*

Sigmund Freud

under the name of Watson's medical colleague and literary agent, A. Conan Doyle. Doyle was an aspiring ophthamologist, who was to undertake his advanced studies at Vienna during 1891, and who must have known of and conceivably even employed cocaine in his practice. Suspicions persist that he was himself an occasional user. There is no direct evidence that he and Holmes actually met, his forty-year association with Watson notwithstanding—in later years Doyle denied ever having set foot in Baker Street—and his rôle, if any, in Holmes's introduction to drugs will probably never be known.

But 1887 is also the most likely year in which Holmes became a "self-poisoner," in Watson's words, by cocaine. The case of *The Five Orange Pips,* the good doctor reports, took place in September 1887, and in terms of occurrence, rather than publication, it bears the earliest mention of drug use on the part of Sherlock Holmes. By July or September of 1888 (Watson mentions both months in *The Sign of the Four*), he had been injecting it three times daily "for many months," yet Watson was just now gathering the courage to remonstrate with him.

"I suppose that its influence is physically a bad one," Holmes admitted with a shrug. "I find it, however, so transcendently stimulating and clarifying to the mind that its secondary action is a matter of small moment."

His tone was typical of the cocaine *habitué,* even of the informed one, and he expressed no idle rationalization, either. By the time of *The Sign of the Four* he had been using cocaine for about a year and achieving practical, tangible benefits—for 1887 had seen him not only taking up the habit but had witnessed the sudden burgeoning of his career after nine years of professional stagnation. His addiction persisted throughout the greater part of his active practice and profoundly influenced it for good and for ill over the years. But it is fair to say that without the initial stimulus of cocaine, there most likely would have been no practice to speak of at all.

And what was the immediate cause of his drug use? There is no sure answer, but it is most likely that he resorted to cocaine for the same reason Freud did—to combat depression.

Dr. A. Conan Doyle

William Gillette as Sherlock Holmes

THE most striking feature of Sherlock Holmes's personality, wrote Dr. Watson time and time again, was its "dual nature." His moods, it was said, alternated between "excellent spirits" and "fits of the blackest depression."

"Nothing could exceed his energy when the working fit was upon him," Watson observed of him in 1881, six years before his recourse to cocaine, "but now and again a reaction would seize him, and for days on end he would lie upon the sofa in the sitting-room, hardly uttering a word or moving a muscle from morning to night."

Holmes displayed distinct manic-depressive traits all his life. When he was absorbed in a problem his nervous energy would sustain the "working fit," but once his mind was unoccupied, depression overcame him: "I have a curious constitution," he said. "I never remember feeling tired by work, though idleness exhausts me completely."

It was out of idleness that he turned to cocaine, as he so clearly put it in *The Sign of the Four:* "My mind rebels at stagnation. Give me problems, give me work, give me the most abstruse cryptogram, or the most intricate analysis, and I am in my own proper atmosphere. I can dispense then with artificial stimulants. But I abhor the dull routine of existence. I crave for mental exaltation."

The manic aspect of Holmes's makeup is largely hidden from modern readers of the Saga. The

American actor-playwright William Gillette, in his 1899 melodrama *Sherlock Holmes,* began the practice of portraying the great detective as a tight-lipped, computer-minded automaton, largely because Gillette himself was a poker-faced fellow smart enough to make a fortune playing himself. He had a flock of imitators, the most successful of whom, Basil Rathbone, shared Gillette's undemonstrative style but not his acting talents. Rathbone and his own successors have preserved on film the shallow, wooden Holmes image to which so many present-day readers are conditioned.

The real Sherlock Holmes, as Dr. Watson described him, may have aspired to emotionless objectivity, but he fell far short of his ideal. Throughout his lifetime he remained high-strung and restless, his excitable nature shooting in a moment to a state of nervous frenzy bordering on hysteria. "He appeared to be in a state of nervous exaltation," Watson remarked of him just before the wild chase down the Thames in *The Sign of the Four.* He was seized with "a purely animal lust for the chase" in *The Boscombe Valley Mystery:* "Men who had only known the quiet thinker and logician of Baker Street would have failed to recognize him." In *A Study in Scarlet,* Watson was "irresistibly reminded of a pure-blooded, well-trained foxhound as it dashes backwards and forwards through the covert, whining in its eagerness, until it comes across the lost scent." His behaviour was nearly hysterical at the conclusion of *The Disappearance of Lady Frances Carfax* and in *The Hound of the Baskervilles* when he realized that the dead man on the moor was not his client. Allusions to Holmes's emotional outbursts in

Watson's chronicles outnumber examples of his self-control by two to one.

Gillette and Rathbone did not invent his exaggerated pose of imperturbability. It was real enough — likely a self-conscious response to his own manic tendencies. Still, Holmes's celebrated composure was a façade that crumbled at the least provocation, and conspicuous instances of his efforts to conceal his agitation may be found in the adventures of *The Dancing Men, The Norwood Builder,* and *The Problem of Thor Bridge.*

To his credit, he did not deceive himself over his depressive attacks. "I get in the dumps at times, and don't open my mouth for days on end," he warned Watson at their first meeting. "You must not think I am sulky when I do that. Just let me alone, and I'll soon be right." Neither does he appear to have been suicidal, though he did display a number of "self-destructive" traits — notably his friendlessness and asocial lifestyle, his ostentatious lack of concern over his fees, and his habit of declining official credit for his successes.

His malady appears to have taken the form of general "melancholia" — listlessness, lack of appetite, feelings of frustration and self-pity — and while the evidence is scanty, it would seem that he was more debilitated by it than one might at first assume. The clues are his early lethargy in pursuing his career and his lifelong expressions of despair over the human condition.

This was depressive withdrawal in an acute form.

Holmes and Watson's first case together, the beginning of the immortal partnership as described in *A Study in Scarlet,* almost did not take place. When invited into the Lauriston Gardens affair by Inspector Gregson, Holmes nearly refused to take it up. "I'm not sure about whether I shall go," he shrugged. "Supposing I unravel the whole matter, you may be sure that Gregson, Lestrade, and Co. will pocket all the credit."

Despite his profession as a consultant, despite Gregson's acknowledgement of his superiority, he petulantly refused to bestir himself to the investigation of a commonplace murder for which he was unable to feel any enthusiasm. His practice at this time was not at all a lucrative one. His livelihood as well as his continued professional connexions depended on just such summonses. Yet had it not been for a desire to impress Watson with his powers, it is possible that he would not have responded at all. This was depressive withdrawal in an acute form.

Less disabling than his apathy, but much more lasting and apparent to a casual reader, was Holmes's continuing pessimism: "The ways of fate are indeed hard to understand. If there is not some compensation hereafter, then the world is a cruel jest," he said in *The Veiled Lodger.* "But is not all life pathetic and futile?" he lamented at the opening of *The Retired Colourman.* "We reach. We grasp. And what is left in our hands at the end? A shadow. Or worse than a

"Was there ever such a dreary, dismal, unprofitable world?"

shadow—misery." His anguish at the conclusion of *The Cardboard Box* might even sum up his life's quest: "What is the meaning of it, Watson? What object is served by this circle of misery and violence and fear? It must tend to some end, or else our universe is ruled by chance, which is unthinkable. But what end? There is the great standing perennial problem to which human reason is as far from an answer as ever."

His bitterness and his egotism kept him, however, from self-reproach. He habitually blamed the world at large for his troubles, a common enough depressive trait: "Was there ever such a dreary, dismal, unprofitable world?" he demanded in *The Sign of the Four.* "The London criminal is certainly a dull fellow," he complained in *The Bruce-Partington Plans.* "Life is commonplace," he sneered at the beginning of *Wisteria Lodge;* "the papers are sterile; audacity and romance seem to have passed forever from the criminal world."

To such a personality, a drug which could deliver him from paralyzing attacks of melancholia would come as something of a miracle. And the fact is that between March 1881, the commonly accepted date for *A Study in Scarlet,* and the year 1887, in which Holmes took to cocaine, Holmes and Watson shared only one case—*The Speckled Band* of April 1883— which the doctor considered worthy of inclusion among the sixty tales of the Saga.

HALL'S COCA WINE
IS A MARVELLOUS RESTORATIVE
In cases of Influenza, Convalescents,
and those suffering from Mental and Physical Fatigue, General
Depression, Sleeplessness, Throat Complaints.

Of Chemists and Wine Merchants, at 2s. and 3s. 6d. per bottle.
or post free from the Sole Proprietors,
STEPHEN SMITH & CO.,
BOW, LONDON.

Portion of an advertisement for Hall's Coca Wine, from the Illustrated Sporting and Dramatic News *(London) of 13 July 1895.*

COCAINE is a powerful stimulant to the central nervous system. Taken by injection, it is still the most effective "upper" known. The user experiences a feeling of great physical strength and considerable heightening of his intellectual powers, as well as a marked indifference to hunger, pain, and fatigue — each of which may be immediately recognized as among the dominant elements of Holmes's behaviour. And the psychological euphoria it produces is a striking, though exceedingly short-term, relief from depression.

Unhappily, it is this contrast between even the mildest depression and the cocaine-induced feeling of indescribable confidence and well-being that is the drug's greatest hazard. Its effects generally last only an hour or two — too transient for any sustained benefit to be realized — and its withdrawal produces an even more severe depressive reaction which the user believes can be overcome only by yet another dose of cocaine. In this way the *habitué* often enough is driven to progressively higher and more frequent dosages in a pattern of psychological dependence as tenacious and as potentially destructive as any narcotic addiction.

In treating of Holmes and cocaine it is important to understand that cocaine is neither a narcotic nor is it physiologically addictive. Unlike opium and its derivatives, morphine and heroin, cocaine does not lull the user into a passive absence of all care. Quite to the contrary, it produces an indomitable self-confidence

Coca leaf

and mental acuity which combine to make one's troubles appear easily surmountable. Physically it is no more enslaving than nicotine or caffeine, its want creating only minor discomfort, with none of the agonizing symptoms of opiate withdrawal nor even the alcoholic *delirium tremens.*

But these non-narcotic and non-addictive qualities of the drug should not be permitted to draw attention from its dangers. As early as 1885 the German authority Emil Erlenmeyer condemned cocaine as "the third scourge of humanity" after alcohol and morphia. It is highly toxic, an undiluted dose of 1.2 to 2.0 grams being promptly fatal. And the toxic effect is cumulative, since the body does not develop a tolerance to progressively higher amounts. Continued use produces an inability to concentrate, delusions of grandeur, and generally erratic behaviour—the first symptoms of "cocaine psychosis," which in its more advanced stages takes the form of paranoia and tactile hallucinations such as the feeling that snakes or insects are crawling upon or beneath the skin.

Unlike other drugs, though, cocaine induces behavioural disorders while the user is still under its influence—in direct contrast to alcohol and the opiates, for instance, the psychotic symptoms of which result not from their presence but from their withdrawal. The reasonably experienced "recreational" user of cocaine has no difficulty in perceiving the drug's adverse effects on himself and in voluntarily moderating or suspending his consumption. Abstention actually produces a cessation of the psychotic symptoms, which do not recur unless its use is resumed and the toxic accumulation in the tissues again builds to dangerous levels.

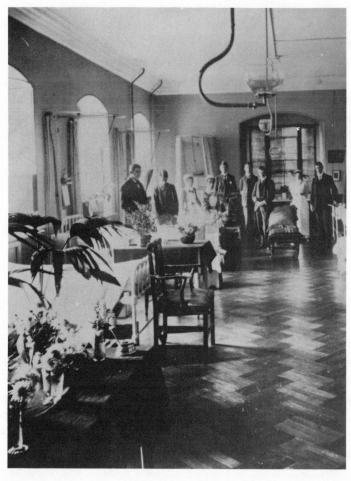

Physicians did not know substantially more about drugs and their effects than did the public at large. . .

HOLMES'S cocaine habit was in no way unlawful. While there were some social stigma attached to drug addiction, much the same as with alcoholism, it did not seriously occur to nineteenth-century legislators to create laws against drug use. Thousands of preparations were sold in stores or made at home in a tradition of folk medicine going back to the dawn of memory. The science of pharmacology, as it is understood today, was in its infancy. Physicians did not know substantially more about drugs and their effects than did the public at large, and paternalistic legislation to shield the citizenry from their own ignorance and "credulous hope" was an idea virtually without precedent before advancing chemical science and advertising technology combined in the 1890s to make apparent the need for statutory safeguards.

Ironically, it was the emergence of cocaine more than any other factor which, in the opinion of many present-day observers, brought about the public outcry against drug-taking. The morphine or opium addict was able to live a normal, worthy life as long as his access to the narcotic was not hampered, and such access had long been a simple matter, since drugs were sold, openly and legally, at uninflated prices, across the counter. But it was cocaine, with its capacity to create bizarre behaviour patterns in active users, which focused attention on drug use and brought into being the popular conception of the "dope fiend."

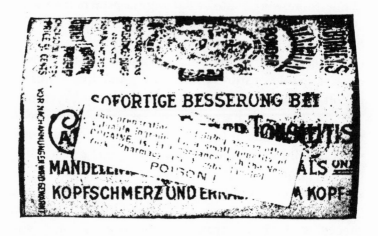

By 1910, most states of the United States had limited the sale
of cocaine to a doctor's prescription. The 1905 New York
state poison label, seen here on a box of Dr. Birney's
Catarrhal Powder (which was actually manufactured in
Germany), reads: "This preparation, containing among other
valuable ingredients, a small quantity of COCAINE, is, in
accordance with the New York Pharmacy Act, hereby labeled
POISON!" Dr. Birney's powder was 4% cocaine.

The popular crusade against harmful drugs in general,
and patent medicines in particular, was led by two national
magazines—The Ladies' Home Journal and Collier's Weekly.
It is hardly a coincidence that Watson suppressed allusions
to Holmes's drug-taking in the stories he wrote during the
first decade of the twentieth century. All fifteen of the tales
published in the United States between 1903 and 1908
appeared in Collier's.

In order to protect the British public from impure or fraudulent supplies, the Poisons and Pharmacy Act of 1908 put cocaine on the schedule of drugs which could be sold only by a registered chemist (pharmacist), but no restrictions were placed upon who might buy them as long as the purchaser was known to the druggist. Not until 1916 was the sale of cocaine restricted to a doctor's prescription. The more comprehensive Dangerous Drugs Act followed in 1920-22. Even today drug addiction is not an offense in Great Britain, and users may purchase their narcotics legally on a prescription "for addiction."

Efforts to cope with the drug problem took a very different turn in the United States, where abuse was admittedly far more widespread owing to the free-wheeling, largely unregulated nature of domestic commerce. Attempts were made as early as 1887 to have the sale of cocaine restricted by law, and by 1910 most states had limited it to a doctor's prescription. The Harrison Narcotics Act of 1914 was intended to regulate, on a national scale, the sale and distribution of narcotic substances, including, mistakenly, cocaine — but the same spirit which resulted in the Prohibition Amendment caused the Harrison Act to be interpreted in the courts as prohibiting *any* possession of such drugs, even by prescription. The result was the *de facto* criminalization of addiction itself, with all the attendant evils of black markets, underworld involvement, and staggering enforcement costs.

But throughout Holmes's era cocaine remained unrestricted by law or custom. It was available in an extraordinary variety of forms — as a snuff, in candies, in coca-leaf cigarettes, as ointments, pills, hypodermic solutions, gargles, "chewing paste," and even suppositories. It was a common ingredient in patent medicines such as "Vin Mariani" in Europe and "Coca-Cola" in the United States.

An Atlanta cough-syrup manufacturer, John Pemberton, conceived Coca-Cola in 1886 as part of a campaign to cash in on the growing coca-beverage market. A year earlier his French Wine Coca ("Ideal Nerve and Tonic Stimulant") had failed to attract attention, and he turned to the "soft," non-alcoholic, drink as an alternative. Coca-Cola ceased to contain cocaine about 1903, but its distinctive, bitter under-taste to this day comes from decocainized extracts of the coca leaf.

Stimulant coca wine was first sold in France in the 1860s and in 1881 was introduced into England, where the editors of the prestigious *British Medical Journal* observed it to be "a very useful nervine stimulant" of value as "a remedial agent in cases of nervous exhaustion, over-study, or excessive mental exertion." Despite their medicinal intent, coca beverages were manufactured and distributed not by pharmaceutical companies but primarily by brewers and wine-dealers. Advertisements were commonplace for such competitive efforts as "dry sparkling coca wine," carbonated cocaine-water ("A Non-Alcoholic Stimulant"), and "coca-bynin," a fluid designed to mix with water or wine so that buyers could prepare their own home remedies.

The most popular of these drinks was "Vin Mariani," the original coca wine as invented by Angelo Mariani, a Corsican chemist and entrepreneur. Over the years Mariani wine acquired a collection of testimonials from an impressive array of celebrities, including composers Charles Gounod (who wrote a little melody

The British Medical Journal

SATURDAY, MAY 28TH, 1881.

REPORTS AND ANALYSES
AND
DESCRIPTIONS OF NEW INVEN
IN MEDICINE, SURGERY, DIETETICS, AND
ALLIED SCIENCES.

COCA WINE.

UNDER the name of " *Vinum Mariani*", Messrs. Robe
introducing into England a preparation of coca pre
leaves of the *Erythroxylon coca*. It forms a very
according to the clinical experience of physicians in Fr
in England, a very useful nervine stimulant. The va
element of economy, as Marvaud has judiciously nam
                in restraining waste, Coca wine is largely prescribed
           and many others. Coca wine is largely prescribed
         it has been found generally valuable as a
       ervous exhaustion, over-study, or exces-
     a certain reputation for enabling athletes
   ithout the usual amount of bod
  considerably to alleviate the dis
  hers who are called upon to make

Dical Journal.

MBER 22ND, 1890.

NIN.
lough Court, Lombard Street,
me of coca-bynin, a combina-
; (bynin) with extract of coca
atable, and mixes readily with
aration of coca wine, and has
o take the wine to which they
xamination shows that coca-
iastasic power, and that the

Analytical Records.

E LANCET.

SATURDAY, AUGUST 6, 1887.

AERATED COCAINE WATER—A NON-ALCOHOLI
(SHILLINGFORD & Co., BICESTER BREWI
  be no doubt of the genuineness
id can readily be separated
roperties observed. A dis
ue was observed in the eve
ion to the bitter taste.
cocaine is the only difficulty in the manu-
s has evidently been effected with due care.

Throughout Holmes's era cocaine remained unrestricted by law or custom.

This extraordinary advertisement for Mariani wine, from the London Graphic *of 11 March 1899, told the literal truth. In a letter to Mariani, Pope Leo XIII's secretary wrote: "Rome, January 2, 1898. His Holiness has deigned to commission me to thank the distinguished donor in His holy name, and to demonstrate His gratitude in a material way as well. His Holiness does me the honour of presenting Mr. Mariani with a gold medal containing His venerable coat-of-arms."*

in praise of it), Ambroise Thomas, and Jules Massenet; sculptor Auguste Rodin; men of letters such as H. G. Wells, Henrik Ibsen, Alexandre Dumas the younger, Jules Verne, and Émile Zola; performers including the English actor-manager Henry Irving, actress Sarah Bernhardt, and Édouard De Reszke the Metropolitan Opera basso (whom Holmes admired in the final paragraph of *The Hound of the Baskervilles*); Popes Leo XIII and Pius X; the kings of Spain, Greece, Sweden, and Serbia; Thomas Edison; and President William McKinley.

"Briefly stated," concluded one 1893 ad for Mariani's concoction, " 'Vin Mariani' is a perfectly safe and reliable diffusable stimulant and tonic; a powerful aid to digestion and assimilation; admirably adapted for children, invalids, and convalescents."

And truth to tell, such puffery was quite accurate. Cocaine does aid digestion. Taken by mouth the small quantities in coca wine were no more harmful than the caffeine present in tea or a child's morning cocoa. Cocaine is a difficult drug to assimilate into the bloodstream. A crystalline powder, it cannot be smoked. It resists dissolving in water. In the digestive system it is detoxified by the liver and too quickly metabolized to provide the sensations sought by the *habitué*.

One effective means of assimilation is through the mucous membranes of the nose — hence the practice of "snorting" cocaine. The only other practical method is by injection.

Holmes's hypodermic syringe must have been similar to this advanced all-glass model introduced in the British Medical Journal *for 8 October 1892.*

THE modern hypodermic syringe was developed in England in the 1850s, and the hypodermic injection of morphia had been commonplace, among both physicians and addicts, for thirty years and more. In the rush of experimentation in the mid-1880s, the subcutaneous administration of cocaine was attempted by 1884 at the latest.

In addition to its use as a local anaesthetic, injected cocaine was found to be effective in weaning patients from the morphine habit, a discovery made largely by Freud himself in 1884. The result, of course, was to transform, in a very short time, a large number of morphine addicts into cocaine addicts. Much more tragic was the drug's use as both a prescribed and a popular "cure" for alcoholism and for smoking.

But it was not long before people were turning directly to cocaine. In a much-publicized speech before the King's County (New York) Medical Society in February 1887, the American specialist J. B. Mattison first warned of the alarming increase in the number of *habitués* exhibiting "pure, primary addiction" to cocaine. Within the year Sherlock Holmes had become one of these.

It should be made clear that Holmes did not take his injections intravenously. "Mainlining" was unknown to the Victorians. Physicians scrupulously avoided injecting any substance directly into a vein, preferring the much slower subcutaneous absorption, and the superiority of the intermuscular technique for avoiding pain, inflammation, and abscess was only just beginning to be acknowledged by the medical community, though it had been recognized for years by morphine users. There was a universal belief that intravenous injection put an undue strain on the system and was to be avoided — as indeed it was in an era when the "germ theory" was still widely disregarded and infection remained a real and constant danger.

The facts that his cocaine use had stabilized at three injections a day "for many months," and that the solutions had grown no more concentrated than 7% during that time, confirm that Holmes was an occasional user whose drug dependence was little far advanced. Such an observation is consistent with his repeated assertions that he had no need of the drug when his mind was occupied during a case, and that he had recourse to artificial stimulants solely as "a protest against the monotony of existence." His was a typical drug-use pattern. Many a taker of "uppers" does so only when he has nothing better to do with himself.

Given his compulsion for excellence in all things, Holmes probably insisted upon cocaine from the firm of E. M. Merck, of Darmstadt, in Hesse, then as now the premier pharmaceutical house of Europe, and even today one of the principal suppliers of commercial cocaine. It was Merck which had begun the drug's manufacture in 1862 and achieved its synthesis in 1885.

Once the need to import coca leaves all the way from South America was eliminated, its cost declined radically. "The prescribers of cucaine [*sic*] have noted with much satisfaction the great reduction in price of the drug which has in recent months occurred," enthused the *British Medical Journal* in November 1886. "Whereas, two years ago, the retail price was two shillings a grain, and even more, the same quantity is now sold for twopence, or even less."

By the rates of exchange then in use, twopence amounted to 4¢ in American currency, and the price of cocaine had dropped to one-twelfth its former value of 48¢ a grain. An apothecary's (troy) grain was equal to just less than 65 milligrams (mg.). If Holmes made use of a 10- to 20-mg. dose in each of his three-times-daily injections, then his habit was costing him between 2¢ and 4¢ a day. Even allowing for the tenfold inflation of the last hundred years, Holmes spent considerably less on cocaine than the average American today spends for cigarettes. Not until the restrictions of the 1920s did cocaine become "the rich man's high."

The drug was commercially manufactured in the form of "cocaine muriate" (cocaine hydrochloride) and sold as a powder. The user was expected to prepare his own mixtures. The 7% solution which Holmes injected was not of unusual strength. Medical men reported therapeutic doses of 4% to 10% and even higher, and 10% became the official strength of solution in the *British Pharmacopœia* in 1898.

Black market "street" cocaine today generally contains 6% to 30% of the drug, though it should be kept in mind that the intravenous administration common now is many times as effective as Holmes's subcutaneous method. "Skinning" cocaine does not provide the distinctive "rush" or "bang" for which the modern-day user resorts to the needle, but a gentler, more subtle suffusion of euphoria as the drug is

Holmes kept his solution-bottle fully exposed on the corner of the mantelpiece.

absorbed into the bloodstream over a period of minutes rather than injected all at once. Considering their relative inconvenience, both the subcutaneous and intermuscular means of injection are considerably less satisfying than the simple "snort," which requires no special devices and involves little discomfort, but which was seldom employed in the nineteenth century.

In *A Study in Scarlet,* Watson described the detective as "rather over six feet, and so excessively lean that he seemed to be considerably taller," and Holmes himself said he was just "six feet high" in the adventure of *The Three Students,* putting his top weight at perhaps 170 lbs. A dose of 20 mg. would be quite sufficient to produce the characteristic euphoria. One grain, or 65 mg. — legally purchased from the neighbourhood chemist — would then provide three ample doses, one day's supply, and a grain a day was often mentioned in the literature of the time as a recommended dosage for the treatment of melancholia.

Holmes might be expected to mix his preparations one or two grains at a time, in a proportion of 7 parts cocaine muriate to 92 parts water to 1 part boracic (boric) acid. One grain in 7% solution has a liquid volume of only about 1 c.c., but because of the danger of spoilage it would have been impractical for him to make up more than a small amount at once.

While powdered cocaine will retain its potency for years, in solution the drug is highly unstable and if exposed to light will decompose in as little as 48 hours. The Victorians had the barest suspicions about the effect of light on chemical compounds, and cocaine spoilage was a frequent complaint of physicians who attempted its use in their practices. Holmes, Watson wrote in *The Sign of the Four,* kept his solution-bottle fully exposed on the corner of the mantelpiece. Further, he had studied organic chemistry at St. Bartholomew's Hospital, which, even as the century was closing, came under attack for failing to teach and practise established principles of asepsis. In the event that Holmes failed to use sterile water in preparing the solution, the cocaine became an ideal culture medium for bacteria which destroyed its effectiveness every bit as quickly as did sunlight.

Each of his injections then consisted of between ¼ and ½ c.c. — depending on the quality of cocaine he was able to buy and the precision with which he made up his solutions — deposited beneath the skin. For this purpose his hypodermic syringe would have to be exceptionally small and finely made, its barrel probably no more than two or three inches in length, as implied by Watson's description of it as possessing a "delicate" needle and a "tiny" piston. Undoubtedly it was made entirely of glass, perhaps even of advanced German design, for it was much too delicate to be of the cumbersome metal construction common at that date.

Depositing anything just beneath the skin by hypodermic is extremely painful, often leaves a scar at the point of injection (as Watson observed of Holmes), and if a sterile needle is not used creates a considerable risk of abscess. As a cocaine *habitué,* curiously enough, Holmes was spared most of the discomfort of such injections. Cocaine itself was an effective local anaesthetic and quickly relieved the needle pain. Moreover, the boracic acid, placed in the solution as an anti-bacterial preservative to retard spoilage, coincidentally acted as a buffer against tissue damage while the cocaine was being absorbed, and served as an antiseptic which prevented the abscesses so common among morphine addicts.

Even when administered subcutaneously, the cocaine would commence to be absorbed into the bloodstream immediately. Holmes began to feel its effects within thirty seconds and remained under its influence up to two hours, after which the depressive reaction began to set in.

In cases of advanced habituation, both dosage and frequency of injection sometimes rose to extraordinary proportions. Dr. Mattison reported that "*habitués* have been known to take it ten, twenty, or more times daily," and as early as 1885 a St. Louis doctor recounted the case of a man who was taking 10 grains (650 mg.) at a dose almost continually. In light of these excesses, Holmes's cocaine use was moderate and even therapeutic.

A morphine addict sketched two days before his death by infection from hundreds of abscessed puncture-points. From The Hypodermic Injection of Morphia *(1880) by H. H. Kane.*

*He was able to overcome his melancholia, rise to his fullest
potential, and undertake the classic cases of his career.*

IT may not be an overspeculation to suggest that cocaine was the salvation of Sherlock Holmes's early career. For nine years—from the beginning of his practice in 1878 until 1887—he had few major successes and was forced to contend with crippling bouts of depression. In 1887, the probable year of his introduction to cocaine, his practice suddenly blossomed with the succession of brilliant triumphs which Watson chronicled in the "ADVENTURES" and the "MEMOIRS." *The Sign of the Four, The Hound of the Baskervilles,* and *The Valley of Fear* all belong to this period as well. He was able to overcome his melancholia, rise to his fullest potential, and undertake the classic cases of his career.

Following his own marriage to Mary Morstan some time during the first months of 1889, Watson's intimate knowledge of Holmes's habits naturally diminished, but it is nonetheless important to note that every single case in which he mentions cocaine by name—there are five of them, detailed in Appendix I—occurred between 1887 and 1889. From *The Man with the Twisted Lip* in June 1889 to the destruction of the Moriarty organization in April and May 1891 there is no mention of drugs in the detective's life.

It must be admitted that, according to *The Final Problem,* Holmes and Watson began to see one another so infrequently that in 1890 they shared only three cases, and that the years 1887-90 are a tangle of chronological inconsistency. Theories of Holmes's drug habits at this time must not be too dogmatic. But this period "at the end of the 'eighties" does correspond with the beginnings of his probe into Moriarty's affairs, providing him with an ongoing puzzle upon which to spend his energies between cases as reported in *The Valley of Fear* and *The Final Problem* — and it is also the period of the repeated successes and professional recognition which were to him the best antidote to depression. It is consistent with the normal patterns of cocaine habituation to believe he may have suspended its use during 1889-91.

Holmes's personality before turning to cocaine is laid out in detail in the second chapter of *A Study in Scarlet*. While this story was published in December 1887, it is well known that it was *written* in April 1886 and that having found a publisher after many rejections its appearance was still held up by Ward, Lock & Co. for over a year. Thus it was written a full year before Holmes's recourse to cocaine, and there is no reason to suspect bias in Watson's sketch of his friend's character during that early period.

His manic-depressive episodes aside, Watson wrote: "Holmes certainly was not a difficult man to live with. He was quiet in his ways, and his habits were regular. It was rare for him to be up after ten at night, and he had invariably breakfasted and gone out before I rose in the morning." This description is in striking contrast with Holmes's behaviour in the "ADVENTURES" and "MEMOIRS."

The precise effects of any substance vary considerably from individual to individual, and for the same individual depending upon the quality of the drug and even the emotional state of the user. Holmes was forever a man of moods and temperament, and his cocainism ultimately spanned a period of more than fifteen years. No one of his many eccentricities can be laid incontestably to drug use—some are demonstrably irrelevant or contrary to such use—but a great many of the personality changes evident in him after 1887 point directly to the characteristic symptoms of cocaine dependence.

Increased physical powers. "Few men were capable of greater muscular effort," Watson wrote in *The Yellow face*, "but he looked upon aimless bodily exertion as a waste of energy, and he seldom bestirred himself save where there was some professional object to be served. Then he was absolutely untiring and indefatigable." That he could have kept himself in training under such circumstances even Watson considered remarkable, attributing Holmes's "fitness" to the sparseness of his diet and austerity of his habits. Cocaine is a more likely explanation.

In this instance, though, the drug only exaggerated his own nervous energy. One of the things Watson observed about Holmes at the first meeting in *A Study in Scarlet* was the strength of his grip, with which one "should hardly have given him credit." "I am exceptionally strong in the fingers," he remarked in *The Beryl Coronet,* and the most extraordinary of all his physical feats was the straightening out of the poker bent by Dr. Grimesby Roylott in *The Speckled Band* a full four years before his cocaine use began.

Insomnia. One of the more singular effects of cocaine is the change it sometimes brings about in the circadian rhythms of the body. The *habitué* will stay awake for two or three or more days at a time and then sleep for a full day. This is a symptom of chronic depression as well, but Watson avers that in the early days Holmes's sleeping habits were regular. After 1887, according to *The Man with the Twisted Lip,* he "would go for days, and even a week, without rest," and even when not on a case he frequently remained up all night, as seen in *The Copper Beeches* and alluded to at the beginning of *The Hound of the Baskervilles.*

Suppression of hunger and thirst. Holmes's neglect of his nutritional needs is legend. His diet, "usually of the sparest," was abandoned altogether when he was working. As with his sleeping habits, though, it is important to distinguish here between his abstinence from food and drink when using cocaine between clients and his failure to eat while distracted by a case. In *The Five Orange Pips* and *The Valley of Fear* he returned famished from his investigations, but in *The Beryl Coronet* he remembered to take a sandwich with him.

Pallour. Abuse of any strong stimulant will produce *asthenopyra,* a low-grade fever resulting from the extended presence of adrenalin in the bloodstream. This takes the form of the pallour and fiery eye so often associated with Holmes. His prodigious consumption of strong shag tobacco would heighten the effect.

Languor. Despite the mental acuity and reserves of physical strength sensed by the user, he nonetheless assumes a "laborious, deep sighing, yawning" attitude of exaggerated repose and "perfect laziness" sometimes verging on rudeness. Holmes's languid, drawling manner as exhibited toward *The Noble Bachelor,* for example, contrasts sharply with the depressive lassitude of *A Study in Scarlet.*

The user assumes a "laborious, deep sighing, yawning" attitude of exaggerated repose and "perfect laziness" sometimes verging on rudeness.

Ocular reactions. Another curious effect of cocaine is its tendency to contract the pupil of the eye (*miosis*), while simultaneously inducing *ptosis,* a drooping of the eyelid, combined with *blepharodiastasis,* an inability to completely close the eye. The result is an unblinking, sunken, "beady-eyed," yet often darting and unsteady stare, disconcertingly at variance with itself and with the relaxed posture of the body—the "minute and yet abstracted" gaze Watson spoke of in *A Case of Identity,* the "weary, heavy-lidded expression which veiled his keen nature" described in *The Engineer's Thumb.*

Loquacity of speech. The first chapter of *The Sign of the Four* is an excellent example of the cocaine user's compulsion to engage in one-sided conversations, to lecture to whomever will listen upon his favourite subject of the moment. Analogous scenes in other stories might be similarly interpreted.

Exaggerated sensory capabilities. "I have. . .an abnormally acute set of senses," Holmes declared bluntly in *The Blanched Soldier* late in his career. His detection of perfume scent on a warning note during the investigation of *The Hound of the Baskervilles* foreshadowed this claim. The many allusions to his sharp eyesight, however, as well as his "extraordinary delicacy of touch," need not be attributed to the drug.

Impotency. While cocaine is almost universally declared to be an "aphrodisiac"—*i.e.,* it makes one highly sensitive to sexual stimuli while under its influence—in men at least, part of the depressive aftereffect is impotency and a prolonged sexual indifference sometimes lasting a month or more. How Holmes might respond to a heightened sensual awareness in the sexually-repressed Victorian age remains an open question, but his cocainism does much to explain the asexual lifestyle stressed in *The Sign of the Four* and *The Copper Beeches.*

Other withdrawal effects. Post-usage symptoms can also include an untoward defensiveness, impatience or irritability, additional insomnia, generalized anxiety, even tendencies to aggressive conduct in some cases of abuse. With the exception of this last, it is virtually impossible to distinguish between the detective's usual high-strung nature and drug aftereffects.

There are some signs of habituation which Watson's sense of Victorian propriety would and did suppress, notably what was then genteelly called "great bodily wasting"—profuse perspiration, watering mouth, running nose, diarrhoea, frequent urination—though not all of these manifestations will appear together in the same person.

Yet another symptom was the occasional failure of Holmes's reasoning powers, still rare in the early days. There were in particular the fanciful conclusions he drew from Henry Baker's hat in *The Blue Carbuncle* and his uncharacteristic leaps to false assumptions in both *The Yellow Face* and *The Second Stain,* early warnings that his cumulative dosage was becoming debilitating. Reinforced by Watson's frequent criticisms, it was a warning he clearly heeded, for there was yet no hint of any lasting interference with his mental abilities. That was to come later.

"The Drug Addict" (1898), poster art by Eugene Grasset

No analysis of Sherlock Holmes's drug use could be complete without a look at the morphine episode of 1888.

The revelation in *The Sign of the Four* that Holmes injected morphine is a startling one at first notice, but in view of the general absence of social prejudice in the nineteenth century and the patterns of drug use as they are now known, the incident assumes more reasonable proportions. Having found considerable benefit from the hypodermic injection of cocaine, he dabbled in other drugs as well.

The Victorians understood nothing of the physiology of addiction, but they learned quickly and empirically that morphine and cocaine were "antithetical." The *habitué's* preference for either the stimulant effect of cocaine or the narcotic effect of the opiate is largely a matter of personality, but hardly anyone uses them both. Once cocaine had become a commonly accessible substance in the late 1880s—the first really powerful stimulant ever to do so—many persons found they preferred the "upper" to the "downer."

Holmes's craving was for stimulation, not for any relaxing of his faculties. Morphine would suppress his ambition, his energies, and his passion for minutae, and that would be intolerable to his singular nature. Moreover, the use of cocaine exaggerates any pre-existing aversion to depressants—hence its early reputation as a "cure" for morphinism and alcoholism —though it must be admitted that the "cure" works both ways, and that morphine proved just as effective in weaning patients from cocaine as the reverse.

The two drugs are occasionally used in combination. A small admixture of morphine dissolved in the cocaine solution is reported to ease the nervous agitation produced by injecting large doses—an unlikely practice in Holmes's case, considering the moderate nature of his habit at this time. Morphine and heroin users sometimes add cocaine to enhance the "rush" sensation of the narcotic—the "speedball" mixture frequently mentioned in drug literature—which, however, not only implies a primary narcotic addiction but which is popular only among intra-venous users, of whom there were none in the nineteenth century. There is no evidence of the "speedball" technique having existed earlier than the 1920s.

During the 1880s in particular, cocaine was abused as an enhancement for virtually every drug then known, including opium, alcohol, and even ether. But once cocaine had come into its own as the most pleasurable of the stimulants, its use in concert with other drugs largely disappeared until after the First World War.

Yet certainly Sherlock Holmes did indulge in morphine during 1888. In addition to the famous allusion at the beginning of *The Sign of the Four,* there are two curious passages in the opening paragraphs of *A Scandal in Bohemia,* which is alleged to have occurred in March of that same year. Holmes alternated "from week to week between cocaine and ambition, the drowsiness of the drug, and the fierce energy of his own keen nature," Watson wrote: "He had risen out of his drug-created dreams, and was hot

"He had risen out of his drug-created dreams, and was hot upon the scent of some new problem."

His disguise as an opium smoker was in the line of duty. . .

upon the scent of some new problem."

These lines are in contradiction not only to
Watson's other descriptions of his friend's drug-
induced demeanor but to cocaine effects generally.
They describe morphine use.

That Holmes kept it up "from week to week" before
March 1888 (or March 1889 according to the revised
dating of a majority of commentators), and was
still at it in (or had been at it since) July or
September 1888, shows that his interest was more
than a casual one—but one understandably abandoned. By the time of *The Yellow Face* in the spring
of 1889, his only remaining vice was cocaine, and no
further mention was ever made of morphine.

His involvements with other drugs were passing
ones. His disguise as an opium smoker in *The Man
with the Twisted Lip* was in the line of duty, and he
quickly assured Watson he had not added opium to
his cocaine habit. His reaction to the hallucinogenic
powder in *The Devil's Foot* was consistent with his
unstable personality, especially in contrast with the
more well-adjusted Watson's milder response to its
effects.

One final drug of interest is nitrite of amyl, which
Dr. Percy Trevelyan of *The Resident Patient* considered useful in the treatment of catalepsy. Amyl
nitrite is not a commonly abused drug, but it is a
useful central nervous system stimulant which at the
same time relaxes the muscles, hence its employment
as a "smelling salt" and the typical Victorian tendency
toward its indiscriminate use as treatment for a
variety of conditions. In the late 1880s some British
physicians briefly considered it as an antidote for the
toxic effects of cocaine.

"I had learned to dread. . .periods of inaction. . ."

FOLLOWING the destruction of the Moriarty organization and his own supposed death, Holmes would have little need for or access to chemical stimulants during his exotic and quite dangerous travels of 1891-94 in Tibet, Persia, Arabia, and the Sudan. It is after his return to active practice in April 1894 that his pattern of dependence seems to have been resumed with nearly disastrous consequences.

The cases Watson dates in 1894 and 1895, most of which appear in the "RETURN" (see Appendix I), are fine specimens of Holmes's work, as good as anything from 1887-91. He would appear to have taken up his career again without a falter—and without the first suggestion of drugs. Then, inexplicably, from *The Bruce-Partington Plans* of November 1895 to *The Veiled Lodger,* "late in 1896," Holmes did not engage in a single case worthy of mention by his biographer. This was the celebrated "missing year" about which commentators have so often speculated.

And in *The Missing Three-Quarter,* treating of events which occurred soon after the end of the "missing year"—December 1896 (Watson's "February" cannot possibly be correct; the Oxford-Cambridge Rugby match was always played in December)— appear Watson's last and best-known remarks about Holmes's cocaine habit:

"I had learned to dread. . .periods of inaction," the doctor wrote, "for I knew by experience that my companion's brain was so abnormally active that it was dangerous to leave it without material upon which to work. For years I had gradually weaned him from that drug mania which had threatened once to check his remarkable career. Now I knew that under ordinary conditions he no longer craved for this artificial stimulus; but I was well aware that the fiend was not dead, but sleeping; and I have known that the sleep was a light one and the waking near when in periods of idleness I have seen the drawn look upon Holmes's ascetic face, and the brooding of his deep-set and inscrutable eyes."

This passage is a palpable falsehood. Holmes's early cocaine use had never seriously threatened "to check his remarkable career," and for the five years 1891-95, possibly since late in 1889, he had been free of the habit altogether. If Watson in fact "weaned" Holmes from some "drug mania," then he did so during the "missing year" just ended.

Watson's statement clearly suggests a debilitating relapse into cocaine use late in 1895, one which kept Holmes from accepting any cases and from which Watson spent the best part of a year retrieving him. Evidently the treatment was not wholly satisfactory. In *The Veiled Lodger,* alone of all the stories from 1894-1902, was Watson not in residence at 221B Baker Street, and one may ponder what circumstances might have driven him, however briefly, from the comfort of his old quarters. "I received a hurried note from Holmes asking for my attendance," he recalled, and quickly responded — expecting, perhaps, a medical emergency, and finding himself drawn instead into one of his friend's cases.

But *The Veiled Lodger* was not a mystery. Holmes pursued no inquiries but merely served as witness to

Eugenia Ronder's confession. Its significance to the Saga is nil, unless it represents a turning point in the detective's life, a moment of empathy between her anguish and his own. "The example of patient suffering is in itself the most precious of all lessons to an impatient world," he argued to her. If Mrs. Ronder's decision not to take her own life in turn inspired Holmes to a resumption of his practice, then this curious little episode assumes an importance indeed.

This new return brought him *The Missing Three-Quarter* and *The Abbey Grange,* two of his most interesting cases both as to events and to Holmes's own indecisive, though ultimately correct, handling of them. His primary affliction remained unaffected, however. Depression — deep, paralyzing, untreatable in the days of pre-psychiatry — demanded the relief obtainable only through cocaine. His rehabilitation lasted less than six months.

As seen in *The Devil's Foot,* he relapsed again in March 1897, when "Holmes's iron constitution showed some symptoms of giving way in the face of constant hard work of a most exacting kind, aggravated, perhaps, by occasional indiscretions of his own." Watson persuaded him to see a specialist, Dr. Moore Agar of Harley Street, who "gave positive injunctions that the famous private agent lay aside all his cases and surrender himself to complete rest if he wished to avert an absolute breakdown."

This time Watson took him away to the desolate moors of Cornwall for a rest-cure which was to last even longer than the "missing year." Sherlock Holmes did not handle a single investigation from March 1897 until the summer of 1898, when he briefly returned to practice with *The Dancing Men* and *The Retired Colourman.*

And then, following the two 1898 affairs, Watson does not positively date a single case before June 1902. Having been reasonably precise about chronology for the more than fifteen years since the partnership began, he suddenly becomes strangely reticent about one of the most eventful periods of Holmes's life. Aside from the bland assertion in *The Solitary Cyclist* that "from the years 1894 to 1901 inclusive, Mr. Sherlock Holmes was a very busy man," mid-1898 to mid-1902 are the obscure years.

A great many of the stories collected in the "RETURN," "HIS LAST BOW," and the "CASE-BOOK" must fall into this phase of the detective's career — the most notable among them being *Charles Augustus Milverton, The Six Napoleons, The Problem of Thor Bridge,* and *The Priory School,* as may be seen in Appendix I. Yet despite these successes, and despite Watson's more and more diffuse allusions to Holmes's personal lifestyle in the later-published cases, examples of his continued drug use stand out.

In *The Dying Detective,* Watson seems almost to take special care in pointing to the hypodermic syringes which littered the mantelpiece in Holmes's bedroom. *The Devil's Foot* is prefaced with the "occasional indiscretions" of 1897, and in *The Creeping Man* mention is made of those "less excusable" institutions in the detective's life which persisted to the very end of his career. Cocaine is still apparent in his unnatural stamina as demonstrated in *The Solitary Cyclist,* the lack of appetite discussed in *The Mazarin Stone,* the insomnia of *The Three Garridebs* and *The Missing Three-Quarter,* the heightened sensory powers of *The Blanched Soldier,* and the growing egomania exhibited in *The Retired Colourman, The Three Gables,* and *The Disappearance of Lady Frances Carfax.*

But it is in the period after 1897 that a new and more distressing element begins to make its appearance — the recurrent signs of advancing cocaine psychosis.

Watson becomes strangely reticent about one of the most eventful periods of Holmes's life.

Holmes begins to exhibit failing judgement and markedly erratic behaviour.

IN a number of the accounts in "HIS LAST BOW" and the "CASE-BOOK," Holmes begins to exhibit failing judgement and markedly erratic behaviour. Most conspicuous is his indulgence in crude and "ill-timed" attempts at humour, as seen particularly in his banter with Steve Dixie and Susan Stockdale in *The Three Gables*. ("Good-bye, Susan. Paregoric is the stuff.") "Holmes's ideas of humour are strange and occasionally offensive," Watson observed candidly at the time of *The Disappearance of Lady Frances Carfax*. In these later years too he developed a vulgar habit of practical joking, his love of simple dramatic effect as seen in *The Naval Treaty* in 1889 having descended by the time of *The Mazarin Stone* to a level of tasteless affrontery. "Perverted," Lord Cantlemere called it.

Equally strange was his lunatic theory of the roots of the Cornish language. "The ancient Cornish language had. . .arrested his attention," Watson wrote, "and he had, I remember, conceived the idea that it was akin to the Chaldean, and had been largely derived from the Phoenician traders in tin. He had received a consignment of books upon philology and was settling down to develop this thesis. . ." In fact, the taking up of queer hobbies may have been one of the first overt symptoms of a toxic breakdown. During *The Bruce-Partington Plans*, his last case before the "missing year," Holmes had become obsessed with the music of the Middle Ages and was

71

hard at work on a monograph about the polyphonic motets of the fourteenth-century composer Orlando Lassus. His Chaldean theory appears in *The Devil's Foot,* the events of which immediately preceeded — or perhaps even accompanied — his second cocaine relapse.

Sherlockians have pointed often to the procedural errors in the later cases, but none are so *outré* as those of *The Disappearance of Lady Frances Carfax.* Having first sent Watson off to the Continent to gather data he could acquire by telegraph more quickly and at a fraction of the cost, and having learned from the doctor that their quarry were returning to England, Holmes then took it upon himself to cross to France, disguise himself as a workman, and spy upon his friend while Lady Frances and her kidnappers lost themselves in London, necessitating the full-scale search which alerted her abductors and nearly cost the lady her life. His utterly bizarre conduct in this affair is typical of cocaine disorientation and carries unmistakable over-tones of paranoia. Its obvious implications for Holmes's course of dependency is that, while in the early years he turned to the drug only between cases, he now used cocaine when actively engaged in an investigation.

This unhappy phase ends on two positive notes. First, despite Watson's frequent silences, 1898–1902 is the period into which some of Holmes's finest performances must fall (see Appendix I), suggesting that his debilitation was intermittent and perhaps not as grave as one might fear. Second, most of the final cases of Holmes's active career — *The Three Garridebs, The Illustrious Client, The Blanched Soldier,* and

The Creeping Man—are once more unambiguously dated, for 1902-3, and are noticeably free of cocaine-related eccentricities.

Over the four years from mid-1898 to mid-1902, then, Holmes engaged in a continuing effort of will against a habit which he recognized as threatening his professional life if not his sanity. Under Watson's care he sometimes shook off the "fiend," sometimes fell back into its clutches. "The relations between us in those latter days were peculiar," Watson concedes in *The Creeping Man,* conjuring up imaginings of a series of relapses, recriminations, and estrangements between the two which are probably more serious than the reality, and which never lasted long in any case. By June 1902, the date of *The Three Garridebs,* he had emerged the winner—and none too soon.

Late in 1902, according to *The Illustrious Client,* Watson once again moved out of the Baker Street flat, and by January 1903 he had married for the second time, "the only selfish action," Holmes complained in *The Blanched Soldier,* "which I can recall in our association." Within the year Holmes had fled to bee-keeping and the study of philosophy upon the South Downs of England.

Without the faithful Watson to support him, and troubled still by his ever-present melancholia, Holmes in the end preferred early retirement—he was only 49 in 1903—to yet another drug relapse which he knew he could not overcome on his own. His gloomy musings on the baseness of mankind at the conclusion of *The Creeping Man* do not begin to convey the pathos of his simple lament in *The Blanched Soldier:* "I was alone."

In contemplative ease upon the Sussex coast. . .

IN contemplative ease upon the Sussex coast, Holmes at last gained some measure of the contentment he had failed to find in cocaine. He made new friends; he wrote, took up swimming and photography, and received an occasional weekend visit from Dr. Watson as he put the records of his past case in order. He had chosen the practical alternative of combating depression by a change of environment, but the final release from his drug need was achieved only at the enormous cost of his very career and the bustling metropolis he had made his life.

The temptation is great to end on a note of optimism, to be reminded of the many incidents in which cocaine took no part, in which Holmes was free of depression and eccentricity, of the triumphal years of his best work and his greatest happiness — and examples abound within the Saga. Yet such a gambit would be artificial and inappropriate to his tragedy.

Still, Holmes's tragedy is not our own. "Work is the best antidote to sorrow," he told his Watson. The same personality which took solace in cocaine found it oftener in action, and without those anomalies of his character there would have been no detective practice, no Holmes-Watson partnership, no Sherlock Holmes legend.

APPENDICES

Appendix I

THE course of Sherlock Holmes's career cannot be divorced from the course of his cocaine dependence. What follows is a reiteration of the chronology of his professional life as related to the drug.

Story titles preceded by an asterisk (*) represent tales in which cocaine is mentioned by name; stories in which the drug or its use are implied or more generally alluded to are marked with a dagger (†); and those in which morphine is mentioned or suggested are preceded by the symbol (‡).

The date preceding each title is that of the case's occurrence, not its publication; publication dates are considered in Appendix II. A bracketed date which follows a title is that given by Watson himself when his stated chronology is rejected by the consensus of Sherlockian chronologists.

Three tales—*The Gloria Scott* (*c.*1873–76), *The Lion's Mane* (1907), and *His Last Bow* (1914)—are outside the scope of this discussion and are omitted from the list.

1878–1886

Holmes's career is struggling and unproductive despite several promising successes which however do little to enhance his reputation; he contends with crippling bouts of depression which threaten to end his usefulness as a detective.

1878

    OCTOBER *The Musgrave Ritual*

1881

    MARCH *A Study in Scarlet*

1883

    APRIL *The Speckled Band*

1887

He turns to cocaine as a means of combating his melancholia.

1887–1891

The classic period of Holmes's career; his most successful and best-known cases occur during these five years. His cocaine use is mentioned often for 1887–89; afterward he may have had no need of the drug in view of his continued triumphs.

1887

    FEBRUARY *The Beryl Coronet*

    APRIL *The Reigate Puzzle*

  * SEPTEMBER *The Five Orange Pips*

    OCTOBER *The Noble Bachelor*

    OCTOBER *The Resident Patient*

1888

    JANUARY *The Valley of Fear*

    SUMMER *The Greek Interpreter*

    AUGUST *The Cardboard Box*

‡ * JULY OR SEPTEMBER *The Sign of the Four*

    SEPTEMBER *Silver Blaze*

    OCTOBER *The Hound of the Baskervilles*

      [October 1889]

1889
‡ * MARCH *A Scandal in Bohemia* [March 1888]
   SPRING *The Copper Beeches*
 * SPRING *The Yellow Face*
   JUNE *The Boscombe Valley Mystery*
 * JUNE *The Man with the Twisted Lip*
   JUNE *The Stockbroker's Clerk*
   JULY *The Naval Treaty*
   JULY *The Second Stain*
   SUMMER *The Crooked Man*
   SUMMER *The Engineer's Thumb*
   DECEMBER *The Blue Carbuncle*
1890
   JULY OR OCTOBER *A Case of Identity*
   JULY OR OCTOBER *The Red-Headed League*
 † NOVEMBER *The Dying Detective*
1891
   APRIL–MAY *The Final Problem*

May 1891–April 1894

Holmes travels in Asia, Africa, and France.

April 1894–November 1895

1894
   APRIL *The Empty House*
   AUGUST *The Norwood Builder*
   NOVEMBER *The Golden Pince-Nez*
1895
   SPRING *The Three Students*
   MARCH *Wisteria Lodge* [March 1892]
   APRIL *The Solitary Cyclist*
   JULY *Black Peter*
   NOVEMBER *The Bruce-Partington Plans*

November 1895–late 1896

The first cocaine relapse; Holmes undertakes no cases as Watson "weans" him from the drug.

Late 1896–March 1897

1896

LATE *The Veiled Lodger*
NOVEMBER *The Sussex Vampire*
† DECEMBER *The Missing Three-Quarter* [February]
1897
JANUARY *The Abbey Grange*
† MARCH *The Devil's Foot*

March 1897–summer 1898

The second relapse; again his professional activities are in abeyance as he struggles to throw off the "fiend."

Mid-1898–mid-1902

The obscure years; brilliant successes alternate with the most erratic personal behaviour, and signs of cocaine psychosis make their appearance.

1898

SUMMER *The Dancing Men*
SUMMER *The Retired Colourman*
1899
JANUARY OR FEBRUARY *Charles Augustus Milverton*
1900
SUMMER *The Six Napoleons*
OCTOBER *The Problem of Thor Bridge*
1901
MAY *The Priory School*

1902

WINTER *The Red Circle*
MAY *Shoscombe Old Place*
SUMMER *The Disappearance of Lady Frances Carfax*

1902-3

Holmes frees himself from the worst influences of cocaine if not entirely from the drug itself. Watson having left him to remarry, he finds himself without his friend's close support in the recurring battle against depression and fears yet another relapse.

1902

JUNE *The Three Garridebs*
SEPTEMBER *The Illustrious Client*
1903

JANUARY *The Blanched Soldier*
MAY *The Three Gables*
SUMMER *The Mazarin Stone*
† SEPTEMBER *The Creeping Man*

Late 1903

Sherlock Holmes retires from active practice.

Appendix II

A STUDY of the tales' publication dates throws an additional light upon the vaguaries of the Holmes-Watson relationship as well as Watson's own response to popular disapproval of drug-taking.

In *A Study in Scarlet* (1887; written 1886), Watson writes of Holmes's periods of depression: "On these occasions I have noticed such a dreamy, vacant expression in his eyes, that I might have suspected him of being addicted to the use of some narcotic, had not the temperance and cleanliness of his whole life forbidden such a notion." By the publication of *The Sign of the Four* (1890), he is remarking with equal candour upon his friend's having taken up the drug habit. The rest of his specific allusions to cocaine, without exception, occur in the "ADVENTURES" and "MEMOIRS," which originally ran in the *Strand* magazine between 1891 and 1893.

When Watson resumed publication of Holmes's exploits after the turn of the century—in America in the anti-drug *Collier's Weekly*—public attitudes toward drugs had changed considerably. He takes care to minimize, if not actually to falsify, the detective's continued cocaine use in *The Missing Three-Quarter* (1904), which appeared at the height of the anti-drug crusade in the United States, and which is the only adventure of the "RETURN" in which drugs are mentioned. His insupportable boast of having "weaned" Holmes from his "drug mania" seems intended as a final word on the matter, after which, he apparently had determined, he would suppress references to drugs.

But he forsakes this attitude in *The Devil's Foot* (1910) and *The Dying Detective* (1913), making thinly-veiled allusions to Holmes's weakness as if perhaps taking some petulant revenge for a falling-out between the two. Both of these stories appear in "HIS LAST BOW," and both were written after passage of the 1908 pharmacy law but before the 1916 act which restricted cocaine sales in Britain. Watson's tactic seems less calculated to injure than to irritate his former companion, but his unkind purpose is no less apparent for that — and the nature of his motive is an intriguing one for speculation.

"He was a man of habits, narrow and concentrated habits, and I had become one of them. As an institution I was like the violin, the shag tobacco, the old black pipe, the index books, and others perhaps less excusable." So Watson remarks in *The Creeping Man* (1923). This is his last reference to Holmes's habit, and, significantly, it occurs in the account of his last professional case. It was not the last which Watson wrote up — he continued to publish until 1927 — but it rather epitomizes the whole tenor of "HIS LAST BOW" and the "CASE-BOOK." He alternates between accounts which enhance Holmes's reputation and those which compromise it with all the irrational spite of an ailing old man.

Their estrangement, such as it was, was an intermittent one. They were reunited for the events of *His Last Bow* in August 1914, and Holmes continued to authorize the publication of his cases until Watson's death, at 75, in 1927. But the partnership, if not the friendship, had long been ended—and cocaine had contributed not insignificantly to its failure. Drug use had led to drug abuse no less tragically in the case of Sherlock Holmes than with far lesser men.

Bibliography

I

Objective and reliable books on cocaine are rare. While others are doubtless forthcoming, these three are presently (1978) the only ones recommended:

Andrews, George, and Solomon, David (eds.) *The Coca Leaf and Cocaine Papers.* New York: Harcourt Brace Jovanovich, 1975.
An anthology of the principal works on cocaine published over the last century.

Ashley, Richard. *Cocaine: Its History, Uses and Effects.* New York: St. Martin's Press, 1975. New York: Warner Books, 1976.
This is the best of the available books, despite Ashley's revisionist belief that cocaine is a benign, if not a beneficent, substance.

Brecher, Edward M., et al. *Licit and Illicit Drugs.* Mount Vernon, N.Y.: Consumers Union, 1972.
The definitive overview of drugs of all kinds, their effects and social implications.

II

A brief listing of the principal contributions to the literature of Sherlock Holmes and cocaine:

Baring-Gould, William S. *Sherlock Holmes of Baker Street: A Life of the World's First Consulting Detective.* New York: Bramhall House, 1962.
Holmes's biographer believes that the detective's nervous collapse of April 1887 *(The Reigate Puzzle)* was directly contributory to his seeking solace in cocaine (pp. 73-74).

Carey, Eugene F., M.D. "Holmes, Watson and Cocaine." *The Baker Street Journal* 13:176-81, 195, September 1963.

Carey, a former police surgeon, argues forcefully and authoritatively that Holmes was indeed a "judicious user" of cocaine, citing a number of the detective's behavioural traits which correspond with his own observations of cocaine *habitués*.

Clark, Benjamin S. "The Final Problem." *The Baker Street Journal* 16:68-69, June 1966.

Holmes invented Professor Moriarty and the 1891-94 hiatus, asserts Clark, as an excuse to go away and cure himself of his cocaine addiction.

Galerstein, David H. "The Dented Idol." *The Baker Street Journal* 21:226-31, December 1971.

"There can be little doubt that this drug did indeed cause a permanent impairment and that Holmes did lose some of those great powers with which he was endowed," Galerstein concludes in an article mostly devoted to enumerating Holmes's failures of judgement and the mishandling of some of his cases.

Goodman, Charles, D.D.S. "The Dental Holmes." *Profile by Gaslight,* edited by Edgar W. Smith. New York: Simon and Schuster, 1944.

Goodman suggests that Holmes employed cocaine only temporarily to relieve the pain of toothache and was never actually a habitual user.

Harrison, Michael. *In the Footsteps of Sherlock Holmes.* New York: Frederick Fell, 1960. New York: Drake Publishers, 1972.

The world's foremost Sherlockian scholar insists that Holmes had "a serious addiction" to "some powerful narcotic," from which Watson's "patient and assiduous attentions" delivered him (pp. 154-55).

McCleary, George F., M.D. "Was Sherlock Holmes a Drug Addict?" *The Lancet* (London), 26 December 1936. *Profile by Gaslight,* edited by Edgar W. Smith. New York: Simon and Schuster, 1944.

McCleary was the first to suggest that "Holmes was pulling the good Watson's leg" in pretending to take cocaine. "The continued use of cocaine leads to degeneration—physical, mental, and moral." Therefore Holmes could not have used it. "The facts can be explained on no other hypothesis."

Meyer, Nicholas. "Sherlock Holmes and Cocaine." *The Baker Street Journal* 24:136-40, 145, September 1974.

The author of *The Seven-Per-Cent Solution* exhorts Sherlockians to accept Holmes's cocainism in its literary and historical contexts. "Thus the real issue here is not whether or not Sherlock Holmes took cocaine, but whether or not we can face the fact."

Miller, William H., M.D. "Some Observations on the Alleged Use of Cocaine by Mr. Sherlock Holmes." *The Baker Street Journal* 19:161-65, September 1969.

Like McCleary, Miller perpetuates the notion that "the cocaine addict is. . .a dangerous and debased person" and that Holmes could not have been addicted to "narcotic drugs."

Naganuma, Kohki. "Sherlock Holmes and Cocaine." *The Baker Street Journal* 13:170-75, September 1963.

Naganuma argues, erroneously, that the hypodermic injection of cocaine was unknown before 1891, and he calls for further investigations.

Smith, Edgar W. "Up from the Needle." *The Saturday Review* 19:13-14, 28 January 1939. *The Baker Street Journal* (OLD SERIES) 2:85-88, January 1947.

Smith agrees that Holmes's cocainism was "sporadic and voluntary" but accepts Watson's statement that he had given it up by the time of *The Missing Three-Quarter*.

[Wolff, Julian, M.D.] "A Narcotic Monograph" [editorial]. *The Baker Street Journal* 13:182-84, September 1963.

Wolff endeavours to correct Naganuma's misinformation.

The text and format of *Subcutaneously, My Dear Watson* were planned by James A. Rock and Jack Tracy.

The composition was performed in 12-point Baskerville on a Compugraphic 88 phototypesetter.

The entire book was printed and bound by the web-offset method by R. R. Donnelly & Sons of Chicago, Illinois.

The paper is creme-white Sebago, sixty pound stock.